Take a Look…

There's Still Money All Around You!

From Hustle to Leverage in the Age of AI

Zangba Thomson

Dedicated to those who believe

opportunity still exists
for those willing to see it.

May you always recognize that possibility,

prosperity, and opportunity surround you—

even in the most unexpected places.

— Zangba Thomson

Table of Contents

Note on the Revised Edition

When *Take a Look…There's Money All Around You!* was first published in 2016, the digital economy looked very different. Artificial intelligence had not yet entered everyday workflows, and many of the tools available to creators today simply did not exist.

A decade later, the landscape has changed dramatically. Automation, AI systems, and the global creator economy are transforming how people produce, distribute, and monetize their work.

Yet the central idea of this book remains the same: opportunity still surrounds those who are willing to recognize it.

This revised and expanded edition reflects the lessons learned over the past decade while preserving the core philosophy of the original work.

Chapter 1

A Decade Later: Opportunity in the Age of AI

How artificial intelligence is reshaping opportunity, leverage, and the modern economy.

We are living through one of the largest technological shifts in human history.

Artificial intelligence is transforming industries, redefining productivity, and reshaping how value is created across the global economy.

When I first wrote *Take a Look, There's Money All Around You!* in 2016, the world was very different.

Artificial intelligence had not yet accelerated into everyday life. Platforms operated differently, entry barriers looked different, and the digital economy had not fully matured.

A decade later, the landscape has changed dramatically. Automation is reshaping industries, AI tools are transforming productivity, and entire categories of work are evolving in real time.

The tools of opportunity have changed, but the principle of opportunity has not.

Despite the technological changes, one thing has not changed: opportunity still surrounds us.

The difference today is that those who understand leverage—especially technological leverage—can move faster, build systems, and create value at a scale that was once impossible.

The tools—and the way value is created—have evolved.

Hustle was the edge.

Today, hustle without leverage is exhaustion.

One evening while working on my publishing platform, I realized how dramatically the landscape had changed. Years earlier, solving a technical issue on my website meant sending emails to freelancers, waiting for responses across different time zones, and hoping someone could diagnose the problem. It could take days before a simple error was resolved.

This time was different. I described the issue to an AI assistant, and within moments it suggested several possible fixes.

The problem that once required multiple professionals was suddenly solvable in minutes.

That moment made something clear to me: the nature of leverage had changed.

Before AI. Before automation. Before the creator economy exploded — the principle was already there.

Opportunity surrounds those who know how to recognize it.

What changed is not the existence of opportunity.

What changed is how value is created.

In 2016, it was the hustle culture.

A decade later, money is derived from intellectual property, distribution ownership, digital leverage, systems over hustle, speed + curation, human judgment amplified by AI. Not just effort.

This new edition reflects that evolution and shows foresight.

A 10-year reflection on opportunity, not just a simple update.

Or a philosophy of opportunity that survived a technological revolution.

It's about reclaiming a narrative territory that opportunity didn't just disappear in the AI era. It multiplied.

Within the decade of writing the first edition in 2016, I've changed since then and so have the world around me.

We lived in a different economic environment back then, but the principles still apply when understood through today's lens.

My focus was simple: recognize opportunity and act on it.

Hustle was the vehicle.

Over the next decade, my perspective evolved.

I watched industries change, platforms rise and fall, and technology accelerate at a pace few people expected.

The principle of opportunity never disappeared—but the way opportunity appears has transformed dramatically.

Before, I mentioned underserved markets, hustle opportunities, service gaps, information arbitrage, local or digital inefficiencies.

Now in 2026: AI compresses skill gaps. Automation reduces entry barriers. Information arbitrage is dead. Content is saturated. Platforms control distribution. Speed outpaces craft.

Opportunity did not disappear in the age of AI—it simply changed form.

It shifted from labor advantage to leverage advantage.

For those willing to understand the shift, this moment in history may contain more opportunity than any previous generation has experienced.

In the past, someone might earn more simply by working longer hours or offering a service locally.

Today, a creator can publish one digital product, build an audience online, and earn from that work repeatedly.

The effort may start the same—but leverage multiplies the result.

The old 2016 assumption:
There is money everywhere if you look.

The new reality:
There is leverage everywhere if you know how to use AI tools.

That's evolution.
This book is not just updates, it's reframing the layers.

The message didn't change. It just got deeper.

Not because the content demands it, but because our authority has evolved, and the landscape has changed dramatically.

From Hustle to Leverage

2016 → Hustle reveals opportunity

2026 → Leverage multiplies opportunity

The first Take a Look… book was written for individuals with a hustle mindset—people motivated to search for opportunities and act on them.

This new AI & Digital Leverage Edition speaks to a broader audience:

- Creators
- Digital entrepreneurs
- Freelancers
- independent media builders
- professionals trying to understand artificial intelligence

In other words, anyone trying to understand where opportunity lives in the modern economy.

That is a larger—and more urgent—conversation.

Artificial intelligence does not eliminate opportunity.

It changes how opportunity appears.

In fact, opportunity did not disappear in the AI era.

It multiplied through leverage.

Hustle may open the door.

Leverage builds the house.

In 2016, hustle and awareness were powerful advantages.

Today those qualities still matter—but on their own they are no longer enough.

The real advantage now comes from combining human effort with technological leverage.

But what exactly is leverage?

Consider a writer working on a book ten years ago. Research often required hours of searching, organizing notes, and drafting outlines from scratch. Today, AI tools can help summarize complex information, organize ideas, and accelerate revisions. The writer still provides the judgment, voice, and creativity—but the tools multiply productivity.

That multiplication is leverage.

Instead of spending days gathering information or restructuring ideas, intelligent tools can assist with those tasks in minutes. This allows creators to focus their energy where it matters most: developing insight, crafting ideas, and producing meaningful work.

Some human qualities remain uniquely valuable:

• empathy
• self-awareness
• moral judgment
• creativity
• intuition

These are qualities AI cannot replace.

But AI tools can amplify what humans already do well. They can help structure arguments, surface counterpoints, generate examples, assist with research, and accelerate the creative process.

Tasks that once took days can now take hours—or even minutes.

And when used wisely, that is leverage.

The Rise of Intelligent Tools

The economic assumptions that shaped the world in 2016 have changed dramatically by 2026.

While the moral principles that guide human decision-making remain the same, the mechanisms through which opportunity appears are evolving at an extraordinary pace.

Artificial intelligence is now becoming one of the most powerful tools available to individuals and organizations.

Entire categories of work are beginning to be automated. Tasks that once required teams of people can now be assisted—and sometimes completed—by intelligent systems.

But history shows that every technological shift eliminates some opportunities while creating new ones.

As certain job roles disappear, new fields and industries begin to emerge. Old job titles fade away, while entirely new ones are created in their place.

This is where opportunity lives. Those who adapt to new tools and learn how to use them effectively will find themselves at an advantage.

In this evolving landscape, average skills alone are often no longer enough.

Increasingly, success comes from combining human judgment, creativity, and discipline with powerful technological tools.

Many industries—such as healthcare, construction, and skilled trades—will continue to rely heavily on human expertise.

At the same time, areas like administrative work, customer service, and routine technical tasks are already being transformed by automation.

The lesson is simple: the tools are changing, and those who learn how to use them wisely will be better positioned to thrive.

The tools may be new, but the principle remains the same:

opportunity belongs to those who learn to recognize and use what is available to them.

I've seen this shift firsthand while running Bong Mines Entertainment.

Tasks that once required coordinating with freelancers, troubleshooting website issues, and spending hours researching solutions can now be assisted by intelligent tools in a matter of minutes.

Artificial intelligence does not replace the vision behind the work, but it can dramatically accelerate the process of turning ideas into finished products.

The Four Human Advantages in the Age of AI

As machines become more capable, the qualities that make humans valuable become clearer.

In the age of artificial intelligence, four human advantages are becoming increasingly important:

Judgment – the ability to make wise decisions when information is incomplete.

Taste – the ability to recognize quality, meaning, and cultural relevance.

Ownership – the ability to build, control, and direct assets, ideas, and platforms.

Systems Thinking – the ability to design processes that allow ideas and work to scale.

As artificial intelligence grows more powerful, these human advantages become more—not less—valuable.

Technology can amplify power, but morality and judgment must guide how that power is used.

I've seen these advantages play out in my own work as a founder and publisher.

While technology can assist with research, editing, and distribution, the decisions about what ideas matter, what stories deserve attention, and how to build something meaningful still depend on human judgment and taste.

In a world increasingly shaped by automation and artificial intelligence, tools can enhance human capability like never before. But tools do not possess **judgment, conscience, or moral responsibility**. Those qualities remain uniquely human.

Artificial intelligence can generate text, automate tasks, and process vast amounts of data. But it cannot make moral decisions, develop authentic taste, or exercise wisdom. That responsibility belongs to people.

In an age of powerful tools, the most valuable human qualities may not be technical skills alone, but judgment, conscience, creativity, and the ability to think strategically about systems.

Those who develop these qualities place themselves directly in the path of opportunity.

The New Opportunity Landscape

Automation is becoming increasingly common across industries. Companies are shifting from labor-intensive models toward systems powered by artificial intelligence and automation.

For many organizations, this transition is part of adapting to a rapidly changing economic environment.

Throughout history, technological shifts have reshaped the nature of work.

Some roles disappear, while new opportunities emerge in their place.

The real question is not whether change is happening—it is how individuals choose to respond to it.

2016 Message:
Work harder. Move faster. Look around. Opportunity is everywhere.

2026 Message:
Work smarter. Build leverage. Use tools. Opportunity compounds when systems replace grind.

That isn't a contradiction. That is growth. And growth strengthens credibility.

The Honest Truth About Hustle in the AI Era

Hustle alone now often gets:

- automated
- commoditized
- outpaced
- underpriced

But hustle combined with leverage can scale. That's where real opportunity begins.

Hustle still matters.

Effort still matters.

But in the age of automation, hustle alone is no longer enough. The new advantage belongs to those who understand leverage.

The chapters ahead explore how opportunity still surrounds us— only now it appears in new forms.

The question is no longer simply whether you are willing to hustle. The real question is whether you are willing to recognize leverage when it appears.

AI Leverage: Moving to the Head of the Table

As the founder and editor-in-chief of Bong Mines Entertainment, I operate inside the modern creator economy every day.

Independent media is what I produce through my digital publishing platform powered by WordPress.

When I wrote the first edition of this book in 2016, artificial intelligence was not yet part of my workflow.

My focus at the time was improving my website—making it mobile-friendly and solving technical issues as they appeared.

To accomplish this, I often relied on professionals from around the world for coding, copyediting, and troubleshooting website errors.

In many ways, my progress depended on the availability of other specialists.

Today, the landscape looks very different.

AI agents can now assist with many of those same tasks.

Instead of coordinating with outside help, intelligent tools can help diagnose problems, generate solutions, and accelerate work that once required several specialists.

Tasks that once took days can now be completed in minutes.

But the real value is not simply speed or affordability. The true advantage is leverage.

By allowing AI tools to assist with technical or repetitive work, creators can spend more time focusing on the areas where human judgment, creativity, and vision matter most.

In many ways, learning how to use AI effectively moves you closer to the head of the table rather than the back of the room.

The difference often comes down to one simple skill: how you communicate with the technology.

In the AI era, the ability to direct intelligent tools is becoming a new form of literacy.

And that brings us to an emerging discipline that is quickly becoming essential in the age of artificial intelligence: prompt engineering.

Prompt Engineering: A New Literacy

In the age of artificial intelligence, knowing how to communicate with intelligent tools is becoming a new form of learning.

The quality of the instructions you give an AI system often determines the quality of the results you receive.

This practice is known as prompt engineering—the art of designing and refining instructions that guide AI systems toward producing useful and accurate outputs.

The way a question is framed, the context provided, and the clarity of the request all influence the quality of the response.

Simply put:

The better your prompt, the better the outcome.

Example:

Weak prompt:
"Write an article about AI."

Stronger prompt:
"Act as a technology journalist and explain how artificial intelligence is changing the creator economy. Provide three examples and keep the tone clear and accessible."

The difference between these two prompts is clarity and direction.

The more context and intention you provide, the more useful the response becomes.

In many ways, prompt engineering is the modern version of asking better questions—and better questions have always been the beginning of opportunity.

The CLEAR Prompt Framework

One simple way to structure effective prompts is to follow a five-part approach called CLEAR:

C — Context

Tell the AI what the situation is.

L—Level or Role

Tell the AI what kind of expert it should act like.

E—Expectation

Explain exactly what output you want.

A—Additional Details

Provide constraints, tone, or format.

R—Refine

Review the result and improve the prompt if necessary.

Example Using the CLEAR Framework

Weak prompt:

"Write an article about AI tools."

CLEAR prompt:

Context: I run an independent digital media platform.

Level: Act as an experienced technology journalist.

Expectation: Write a 700-word article explaining how AI tools are helping creators work faster.

Additional Details: Use simple language and include three real-world examples.

Refine: After generating the article, suggest a stronger headline.

Why This Matters

Learning how to communicate with artificial intelligence is simply another way of recognizing opportunity.

The tools may be new, but the principle remains the same: those who learn to see possibilities where others see obstacles will always find ways to create value.

In the age of automation, opportunity has not disappeared—it has multiplied. The difference now is that those who understand leverage, technology, and creativity will be able to capture more of it than ever before.

As powerful as AI tools have become, technology alone is not the real advantage. The true advantage belongs to those who understand how to combine awareness, judgment, and leverage.

In the chapters ahead, we will explore how opportunity still surrounds us—how to recognize it, how to act on it, and how to build systems that allow it to multiply.

The tools have changed.

The principle has not

There is still money all around you.

But before any tool can multiply opportunity, a person must first recognize their own ability to create value.

Chapter 2

The Moneymaking Machine Within You

Recognizing your ability to create value in any environment

2026 Perspective: In an economy increasingly shaped by automation and digital tools, recognizing your own ability to create value has never been more important.

In the previous chapter, we explored how technology and artificial intelligence can multiply opportunity. But before any tool can amplify success, a person must first recognize their own ability to create value.

It's true what they say:

"You can lead a horse to water, but you can't make it drink."

This ancient proverb applies to everyone under the sun; so, throughout this book, you will be given several key ingredients that will help you unlock that moneymaking machine inside of you, but it's going to be up to you to put them to use.

Your success begins, continues, and ends with you.

You are the master key to your success.

You are the main ingredient in your life.

Only you can get up and walk on that hard road to prosperity. No one can do it for you, but you.

You are, and will always be, the captain of your ship, the boss of your thoughts, and the master key that opens the door to you becoming a prosperous creator of value.

You set the wheels in motion, but no one ever said that it would be easy to accomplish your goals or dreams.

Rest assured, nothing substantial in life will ever be handed to you on a silver platter.

You have to go out there and work hard for what you want like everyone else.

Stop waiting for someone to give you that big break.

You came into this world with a vision, and over the years you've nurtured that vision inside of your mind. And now the time is ripe for you to live it.

Do not delay another moment because time waits for no one.

Opportunity sometimes knocks only once, and then it disappears, hopefully to reappear again; therefore, use your time wisely.

Work hard but work smart. Hone your talent, and after you have overcome every obstacle in your way, you will realize that your impossible dream wasn't so impossible after all.

Then your confidence will begin to grow, and your name will glow in bright, star-studded lights.

The world will finally see that you are a force to be reckoned with.

But before that happens, there are things that I want to share with you—key ingredients that will help you to become a producer of prosperity.

It's not by coincidence that you are reading this book. I wrote it just for you and everyone else who have a vision of becoming prosperous.

But the first thing I want you to realize is that the "money" that's written in the book's title, *Take a Look... There's Still Money All Around You!*, can actually mean anything that you want it to mean.

It can mean money, love, friends, opportunities, or whatever your heart yearns for because everything in this world is connected.

I chose money because of its universal importance, and arguably, what materialistic thing has our civilization made that's more appealing than money?

When you begin to realize that you are the master key to becoming prosperous, you will start seeing opportunities everywhere.

The old workout machine collecting dust in your home gym or the extra pairs of sneakers sitting in your closet suddenly become items you can sell online.

Services that you've been doing for free for many years can suddenly become services people are willing to pay for—especially today when digital platforms make it easier than ever to offer skills and reach customers around the world.

In many ways, money really does grow on trees. A large portion of U.S. currency is made from cotton.

Cotton comes from a plant, and that plant produces the fibers used to manufacture paper currency. In other words, something that begins in nature eventually becomes money.

The same principle applies to you. Your ideas, talents, and services are like seeds. When cultivated and developed, they can grow into something valuable.

Just as a farmer turns crops into income, you can turn your abilities into prosperity.

Today, digital tools and artificial intelligence can help those ideas grow even faster—but the seed still begins with you.

Now, your ideas can travel farther than ever before through digital platforms, automation, and artificial intelligence.

Everything you envision—your ideas, talents, and services—should be viewed the same way a farmer views his crop.

In today's digital economy, those crops can grow far beyond your local environment, reaching audiences and customers across the world.

Now, ask yourself, "How much money can I make from this idea of mine, from this service that I am offering, or from this talent that I have?"

The answer should be a set amount that you want to receive, in exchange for the service or product that you are offering.

Imagine being all that you can be and yielding the fruits that your ideas or talent produce.

20

You will lack nothing but gain everything in return because you will be using your abilities to become prosperous.

The tools available today—from digital platforms to artificial intelligence—can accelerate opportunity in ways that were unimaginable just a decade ago. But the seed of prosperity still begins with the individual who recognizes their own ability to create value.

You might say, "Brother Zangba, I don't have the athletic ability of a Kobe Bryant or LeBron James, the business instincts of a Warren Buffett, or the inventive genius of a George Washington Carver or Steve Jobs. Can I still build a prosperous life?"

Yes, you can. Each of those individuals succeeded by developing their own unique gifts. And just as no two snowflakes are identical, every person has abilities that can be cultivated into something valuable.

Throughout the day, repeat this to yourself:

I am a prosperous moneymaking machine.

I see opportunities all around me.

Say it often enough and your mindset begins to change.

Faith comes by hearing.

Pretty soon, you will start believing that you are indeed a producer of prosperity, and that's when the magic happens.

Soon you will begin to see opportunities everywhere you look— even in places where others see nothing at all.

But there are key ingredients I want to share with you—principles that, when combined and applied, can help you build a prosperous life.

When you finally recognize the moneymaking machine within you, something remarkable happens—you begin to see opportunities everywhere you look, and you realize that there truly is money all around you.

Chapter 3

Knowing Is Half the Battle

Why knowledge reveals opportunity

"If I have potential, what do I do next?"

The answer is simple.

Acquire knowledge.

Once you recognize your ability to create value, the next step is understanding how the world around you works. Knowledge is often the difference between seeing an opportunity and missing it entirely.

Today, knowledge is more accessible than at any other time in human history. Books, experienced mentors, and even intelligent digital tools can help accelerate the learning process—but the responsibility to seek knowledge still belongs to the individual.

In many ways, the modern ability to ask clear and thoughtful questions—whether to people, books, or intelligent tools—is simply another way of pursuing knowledge.

I first heard the phrase "knowing is half the battle" while watching the animated TV miniseries *G.I. Joe: A Real American Hero* in the mid-1980s.

Each episode ended with a short public-service announcement where the G.I. Joes helped children navigate everyday problems and offered simple but powerful lessons. Some of those lessons stuck with me.

Lady Jaye once said, "It's okay to be a chicken if you're smart. There's nothing chicken about being smart. If you stop and think, there's almost always a better way."

Another message encouraged kids to face problems directly instead of avoiding them. The point of those moments was simple: Awareness and knowledge help people avoid mistakes and make better decisions. The show ended those lessons with a phrase that has stayed with me ever since.

Knowing is half the battle.

Long before television shows were teaching children this lesson, military strategists understood the same principle: knowledge and awareness determine the outcome of most battles.

"If you know the enemy and know yourself, you need not fear the result of a hundred battles…"

— Sun Tzu, The Art of War

Sun Tzu's message is simple but powerful: awareness determines advantage. If you understand the environment you are operating in and you understand your own strengths and limitations, you dramatically increase your chances of success.

The same principle applies to opportunity.

When you understand how the world works and what you are capable of contributing, you begin to see possibilities that others overlook.

Strategy, whether in war, business, or life, begins with awareness.

Are you aware that whatever it is you are searching for may already exist, waiting for you to discover it? But to obtain it, you must give something of value in return—an idea, a service, or a solution.

Anything substantial that you want to achieve in life—whether it's obtaining a college degree, opening a business, or simply baking a cake—requires knowledge and preparation.

Everything there is to know about the field that you are venturing into must be acknowledged. Once that knowledge has been obtained, you have already won half the battle.

But let's pause for a moment and consider what the word knowledge truly means.

Knowledge is the foundation of progress.

It is the understanding gained through study, experience, and observation.

In many ways, knowledge can also mean understanding yourself: knowing what you can do, what you cannot do, and where your strengths and limitations lie.

In Ayn Rand's 1957 novel *Atlas Shrugged*, one of its central characters, Francisco d'Anconia, poses an interesting question:

"Have you ever looked for the root of production? Take a look at an electric generator and dare tell yourself that it was created by the muscular effort of unthinking brutes… Try to grow a seed of wheat without the knowledge left to you by men who had to discover it for the first time… and you'll learn that man's mind is the root of all the goods produced, and of all the wealth that has ever existed on Earth."

The beginning of all things is knowledge.

Before ideas become action and plans become results, knowledge must come first.

In other words, every product, service, and innovation begin with knowledge and an idea formed in the human mind.

Before the plant (you) produces cotton (your ideas or services), long before the harvest (earnings or rewards), even before a single seed (your plan or strategy) is planted in the ground of your mind, knowledge must first take root.

Knowing what to do—and the correct way to go about doing it—is extremely important.

But how is knowledge obtained?

By reading books, studying your field, or seeking guidance from experienced professionals who have already traveled the road you are about to take.

Once that knowledge is obtained, the next step is to develop a plan or strategy for how to apply what you know—including an honest understanding of what you can and cannot do. Then you must move forward with confidence and execute that plan until your goal is within reach.

Knowledge and strategy give you direction—but persistence gives you momentum.

Do not be afraid of obstacles. Along the way you will encounter unexpected challenges—moments that may tempt you to quit.

Do not allow negative emotions to take control. There is almost always a way through any difficult situation.

This is the secret: whenever you encounter an obstacle, change for the better, and your situation will begin to change as well.

Do not remain stagnant, especially in a world that is constantly evolving.

Expect to fall from time to time, but every time you fall, get back up.

Failure is not falling down.

Failure is refusing to get up.

Recovering from setbacks takes time, courage, and patience.

During those moments, take the opportunity to reflect on what happened, what went wrong, and what could be done differently next time.

Successful people have fallen more times than their fingers can count, but they rise each time with greater experience and understanding.

In the future, you will likely fall again—but that is not something to fear. Every setback carries a lesson, and those lessons gradually build wisdom.

That wisdom becomes one of your most valuable assets because it sharpens your judgment and helps you recognize opportunities that others overlook.

That is why experienced candidates are often chosen first during job interviews. They have already learned lessons through trial and error, while an inexperienced candidate is just stepping into the pool for the first time.

Knowledge in Action

Knowledge becomes powerful only when it is applied.

Once you understand something—whether it is a skill, a business opportunity, or a new idea—the next step is to put that knowledge into motion.

Study the field you are entering, learn from people who have already succeeded in it, and observe how things actually work in the real world.

Knowledge gives you direction.

Experience gives you wisdom.

Action turns both into results.

Author Veronica Roth once wrote:

"No matter how long you train someone to be brave, you'll never know if they are or not, until something real happens."

Life works the same way. When you experience challenges and setbacks, you begin to reveal who you truly are and what you are made of.

Some people repeat the same mistakes over and over again. Others learn from those mistakes, grow stronger, and eventually become the ones who succeed.

They may fall many times—some falls more painful than others—but they rise each time with greater wisdom and experience. And because they learn from those moments, they begin to recognize opportunities that others fail to see.

When I first heard Donnie McClurkin's song *We Fall Down*, I appreciated its simple but powerful message: *we fall down, but we get up.*

That message applies to life as well. When obstacles appear and everything seems uncertain, you must find the strength to rise again.

Every time you rise after a fall, you build confidence. And confidence is one of the key ingredients needed to become a prosperous moneymaking machine.

Confidence allows you to perform at your best. It gives you the courage to keep moving forward and to pursue the opportunities that surround you.

Now that you understand the role knowledge plays in success, you have already won half the battle.

The next step is to use what you know—move forward with confidence.

Make your next move your best move.

Chapter 4

Turn Your Line of Credit into Your Financial Ally

Understanding how financial tools can work for you instead of against you

When I was in high school, I took credit for granted and maxed out my first credit cards within months of receiving them.

At the time, I didn't fully understand how important good credit was, and no one had taught me how to build it responsibly.

I only learned that lesson after graduating, when I applied for an auto loan and was denied. The letdown weighed heavily, but I only had myself to blame.

Instead of building my credit during those early years, I had foolishly turned it into a financial burden.

When I couldn't afford to repay the debt I had accumulated, I fell into the red, and collection agencies began calling endlessly.

I tried to avoid their calls the best way I knew how, but the fact remained: I had created a financial problem, and it was my responsibility to fix it.

At that point, my credit score was in the low 400s, which made me a high-risk applicant.

I desperately needed to repair my credit because I had treated my line of credit like imaginary money.

Since it had come so easily, I failed to value it.

I spent recklessly on nonessential items such as clothing and sneakers—things that quickly lost their value.

Meanwhile, my credit-card debt continued to grow. Each month that I ignored calls from bill collectors, the balance increased, and the problem became even harder to fix.

Back then, employers weren't checking prospective employees' credit history, so I wasn't in jeopardy of losing out on a minimum-wage job.

Still, it took me several years to eliminate my debt, and each payment served as a steady reminder of the consequences of mismanaging credit.

I struggled financially for a while, and eventually I decided that I had to reverse my self-inflicted misfortune.

The first step was obtaining the proper knowledge about how credit actually works.

I read books and consulted financial professionals.

After paying off my debt, I realized that I had almost no credit history left because so much time had passed without any credit activity.

So, I took what I had learned from books and credit experts and developed a simple plan to rebuild my credit, despite my earlier mistakes.

It took lots of patience, discipline, and sacrifice to get back in credit shape. But I knew if I was to stay afloat, I had to play by the rules.

The first thing I did was something I never did before, which was following a strategic game plan.

The first card I applied for was a BP gas card, and I was approved for a $300 line of credit.

Even though the amount was small, I knew that if I could successfully manage a small account, larger opportunities would follow.

But here is an important rule to remember:

try to keep your balance below roughly 30 percent of your credit limit.

Credit scoring systems reward disciplined borrowing and responsible repayment.

I followed this rule faithfully and paid my bill each month, without one single late payment, and when my balance was paid off, I purchased more gas and continued adding necessary data to my credit history.

After several months, I moved on to phase two, which was obtaining another credit card. This time, I wasn't searching for opportunity. It showed up at a Macy's cash register. I was standing in line ready to make a purchase when the cashier asked, "Would you like to apply for a Macy's credit card?"

I thought about it for a moment and replied, "Why not?"

Deep down, I wasn't sure if I would be approved because of my past credit history.

In fact, I expected to be denied.

But after a few minutes, the cashier said, "Wow, it went through, and you've been approved for $500 in store credit!"

She was extremely happy because my approval gave her the first credit account she had opened that day, putting her one step closer to meeting her daily quota.

I breathed a sigh of relief and thought about all the months I had successfully managed my BP card.

My strategy was finally beginning to pay off.

Even though it was a small victory, it meant a lot to me. That day I paid 90 percent of the purchase in cash and placed the remaining 10 percent on my new Macy's card, which I paid off using the same strategy I used with my BP gas card.

I felt a sense of accomplishment, and shortly after that financial victory, I moved on to phase three, which was obtaining another credit card to help boost my credit score.

This time, just like before, another opportunity appeared at a Best Buy cash register.

I was purchasing a handheld gaming console, and just like my Macy's trip, I had the cash ready. But then the cashier asked, "Would you like to open a Best Buy credit account?"

With confidence I said, "Let's do it!"

He checked my credit, and within minutes I was approved for a $2,500 line of credit.

When the cashier told me the credit limit, I could hardly believe it.

So, I asked, "Can you say that again?"

He repeated, "$2,500!"

That's when I realized the strategy was working, and the key was to stay disciplined and continue following the plan.

Just like before, I paid 90 percent of the purchase in cash and placed the remaining 10 percent on the new Best Buy card, which I paid off using the same strategy I used with the BP and Macy's cards.

Around that time, I discovered Credit Karma, a platform that provides free credit monitoring, score tracking, and financial insights. Tools like this can be powerful because they allow people to see how their financial behavior affects their credit over time.

After signing up, I was surprised to see how much my credit had improved. I was no longer in the low 400s. My credit score had climbed to 660, according to TransUnion. It had taken about a year and a half of disciplined payments to get there.

One of the helpful features of the platform was that it suggested credit cards with strong approval odds based on your credit profile. I decided to try one of those recommendations and applied for a Discover It card. At that point, I already had two store cards and a gas card, so expanding my credit profile made sense.

After submitting the application through the platform, I was prompted to call Discover to verify my information. Once I navigated through the automated system and spoke with a representative, I was told that I had been approved for a $7,500 line of credit.

I could hardly believe it, so I asked the representative to repeat the number. "$7,500, sir," he confirmed.

In that moment, I realized how powerful disciplined financial habits can be. Not long before, I had struggled to qualify for basic credit accounts. Now I had access to a substantial line of credit because I had followed a disciplined strategy.

A few months later, I was approved for another card with a $9,500 limit, further strengthening my credit profile.

Today, technology makes monitoring and managing credit far easier than it once was.

Digital financial platforms allow individuals to track their credit scores, receive alerts, and better understand how borrowing behavior affects their financial reputation.

Access to this information gives people the ability to make smarter financial decisions and build stronger credit over time.

Sometimes the opportunity around you isn't a business idea—it's simply learning how to use the financial tools already within your reach.

Looking back, I realized that everything changed once I gained the right knowledge, created a clear strategy, and executed it with discipline.

Credit, when used responsibly, is a financial tool that can help individuals build stability and expand opportunity.

In today's digital economy, access to responsible credit can also function as leverage.

Entrepreneurs, creators, and small business owners often use credit to invest in tools, education, and technology that expand their productivity.

The key is not simply having credit but knowing how to use it wisely.

When used responsibly, credit is not simply borrowed money—it is access. Access to opportunities that might otherwise remain out of reach.

A strong financial reputation can open doors to better interest rates, business funding, investments, and entrepreneurial ventures.

In many ways, credit is another reminder that opportunity often exists in places we overlook. Just as ideas can become income, financial tools can become leverage when used wisely.

Chapter 5

Live Within Your Means

Why Discipline Is the Foundation of Financial Stability

One of the most important financial lessons a person can learn is surprisingly simple:

do not obtain what you cannot maintain.

A friend once shared that advice with me, and the statement stayed in my mind for years.

At the time, I didn't fully understand its meaning. But as I gained more experience managing money, I realized that he was talking about something fundamental—living within your means.

Living within your means is the practice of understanding what you can afford, what you can sustain, and what responsibilities you are prepared to carry.

When spending consistently exceeds income, financial pressure begins to build.

Over time, that pressure often turns into debt.

Learning to live within your means is not about limitation. It is about discipline. It is about creating stability so that the money you earn works for you rather than against you.

Many people today find themselves living paycheck to paycheck, constantly trying to keep up with rising expenses. But it doesn't have to be that way. With discipline and awareness, it is possible to live within your means and begin saving time, energy, and—most importantly—money.

For many people, managing money is like placing cash into a wallet with holes in it—no matter how much goes in, it slowly slips away. But the good news is that those holes can be patched. With discipline, awareness, and a clear plan, you can begin protecting the money you work so hard to earn.

Let's say you make $3,200 a month. After paying your rent or mortgage and other essential bills—such as electricity, water, transportation, and groceries—you may still have a portion of your income remaining.

One smart approach is to divide that remaining money intentionally. For example, you could place **10 percent into savings** and **15 percent into investments**, while using the remaining portion for everyday expenses. Even small amounts set aside consistently can grow over time and create financial stability.

In many ways, you are creating your own personal savings plan. The sky isn't the limit, it's only the beginning, and you can define your own financial boundaries by setting limits to your unnecessary spending habit.

Remember, you are a prosperous moneymaking machine. But in order to safeguard the money you earn; you must learn how to manage it wisely.

That knowledge can come from reading money-management books or seeking guidance from financial professionals.

In addition to gaining knowledge, you must also strengthen your willpower. Learn how to say, "No, I don't need this," or "No, I don't need that," and focus your spending on the things you truly need.

The simple life is the best life.

This basic concept, when it solidifies or becomes a habit, will help you become the most productive version of yourself. But I know it's easier said than done, and that's why you have to exercise your higher self, to overcome your material wants and temptations. You have to know how to defeat your unnecessary spending thoughts, by throwing them in the sea of no return.

Every day new products are introduced to the market, and it is easy to feel tempted to buy them. There is nothing wrong with enjoying the things you like—**if you can afford them**. But when purchases are driven by impulse rather than discipline, people quickly find themselves living beyond their means.

I remember growing up in Jamaica, a neighborhood in Queens, New York, during a time when hip-hop was rapidly emerging as a powerful cultural force. The climate was extremely vibrant, like many urban communities along the East Coast. Fashion and personal style were an important part of the culture, and many young people paid close attention to the clothes and sneakers they wore.

Around that time, my sister and I were being raised solely by our mother. She always made sure we looked clean and presentable, and for that I am extremely grateful.

But there were times when I wanted things we simply couldn't afford—moments when I wished I had the same designer clothes the rappers on TV wore or the sneakers the basketball stars promoted.

I remember wanting Magic Johnson's Converse sneakers when they came out in 1988. At the time, they felt like the pair every kid wanted. But the price tag was beyond what my mother could afford. So, this is what she did: she bought me a basic gray-and-white pair from Models. Even though they weren't the Magic Johnson pair I wanted, they were still part of Converse's classic All-Star line. I wore them to school with pride every single day because I was grateful to have a new pair of sneakers, even if they weren't the ones I originally wanted.

I didn't realize it at the time, but my mother was teaching me an important lesson about living within my means.

Looking back now, I understand that those early experiences were teaching me something far more valuable than a pair of designer sneakers—they were teaching me discipline.

The same discipline that helped me appreciate what I could afford as a child eventually shaped how I learned to manage my money as an adult.

Once you understand where your money is going, the next step is deciding where your money **should** go.

One simple budgeting framework that has worked well for me is what I call the 10 / 15 / 75 Rule, an idea I first came across on the Minority Mindset YouTube channel.

It divides your income into three priorities: protecting your future, building opportunity, and covering everyday living expenses.

Pay Yourself First – The 10 / 15 / 75 Rule

• 10% – Savings

Money set aside to grow over time.

• 15% – Investments

Funds reserved for opportunities and investments.

• 75% – Living Expenses

Money used for bills, food, clothing, transportation, and entertainment.

This simple structure helps ensure that your future is always funded before your lifestyle expands. Even if the amount is as small as **ten dollars**, I still follow the same process and divide the money according to this structure. Over time, this simple practice builds discipline and creates one of the most powerful financial habits you can develop, which is learning to **pay yourself first**.

When you consistently pay yourself first, you begin to build a financial foundation that helps you live within your means while preparing for future opportunities.

Robert T. Kiyosaki, author for the *Rich Dad Poor Dad* series, wrote:

"Pay yourself first."

This simple idea reflects the power of financial self-discipline.

Likewise, George S. Clason, author of *The Richest Man in Babylon*, wrote a timeless principle:

"A part of all you earn is yours to keep."

Both of these ideas point to the same powerful habit: before you pay bills or spend money on everyday expenses, set aside a portion of your income for yourself.

Paying yourself first means directing a percentage of your income into savings or investments before anything else.

When you do this, you are making a clear statement about your financial priorities—you are saying that your future comes first.

The first step to living within your means is developing the willpower to say no to unnecessary spending.

The next step is understanding where your money is actually going.

One simple way to do this is by writing down your income and tracking your expenses.

In many ways, this process creates a **budget**, which is simply a plan for how your income will be used over a period of time.

A budget helps establish spending boundaries and prevents unnecessary debt from accumulating.

Just as the ocean has natural limitations that keep its waters contained, your finances also require structure.

Setting clear spending limits helps prevent small expenses from gradually turning into unnecessary debt.

Financial peace often comes from balance.

When you manage your money wisely, stress begins to fade, and stability begins to grow.

Living within your means is not about limitation—it is about control.

When you develop the discipline to manage what you earn, you place yourself in a stronger position to recognize and take advantage of the opportunities that exist all around you.

Once you learn to manage the money you earn, the next step is learning how to invest in the person who earns it—you.

Chapter 6

Invest in Yourself

Why your skills, mindset, and character are your greatest assets

Legendary investor Warren Buffett once said something profound about the value of investing in yourself:

"Investing in yourself is the best thing you can
do."

Powerful things begin to happen when you invest in yourself—your time, your energy, your knowledge, and your character.

In today's rapidly changing world, investing in yourself has become even more important.

Technology, artificial intelligence, and automation are transforming industries at an incredible pace.

Tools may become smarter, and systems may become faster, but the most valuable asset will always be the person who knows how to think, learn, adapt, and create.

The more you develop your knowledge, judgment, and character, the more valuable you become in any economy.

Think of your body as the vehicle and your mind as the engine that drives it. The condition of that engine determines how far you can travel on the road to prosperity.

When you invest in strengthening your mind and caring for your body, you increase your ability to create value in the world.

Crucial things, such as eating right, exercising regularly, meditating, and getting the proper rest, are all necessary ingredients in maintaining the health of your mind, body, and soul.

What you put in is what you're going to get out.

Over the years, I've come to realize that the greatest investments a person can make are not always financial.

Many of the most valuable investments are the ones you make in yourself.

The twelve investments that follow can be grouped into three important areas of personal development: **mental discipline, personal strength, and practical action**. Together, these habits strengthen your ability to grow, create value, and recognize opportunity throughout life.

These are not financial assets you place in a bank. They are lifelong personal advantages—habits and qualities that strengthen your mind, build your character, and increase your ability to create and recognize opportunity.

Mental Discipline

Habits that strengthen how you think.

1. Invest in Patience

Patience is the ability to endure delays, difficulties, or frustration without losing control. It cannot be purchased, rushed, or borrowed from someone else. You cannot walk into a store and buy patience. It must be developed over time through practice, reflection, and experience.

Learning patience is rarely comfortable. There will be moments when frustration takes over and you lose your composure. That is part of the process. Growth often requires repetition, discipline, and time. Very few meaningful things in life happen overnight.

One of the places where I learned patience was in my garden.

Gardening forced me to follow nature's clock rather than the clock on my wrist. Seeds do not grow faster because you want them to. They grow according to their own rhythm. That realization helped me see a connection between a gardener and an author. Both operate with what I like to call a **planter's mindset**.

A gardener plants seeds and nurtures them for months before the first signs of growth appear. An author plants words onto a page and nurtures them until an idea eventually becomes a finished story. In both cases, the results take time to appear. Before plants bear fruit and before a book reaches readers, patience must first do its quiet work.

Maintaining a garden also taught me something unexpected. Removing weeds required careful attention and consistency. At first, I found the task frustrating. But over time, I began to see it differently. Pulling weeds from the soil reminded me of removing unproductive thoughts from the mind. Both require awareness, discipline, and patience.

Eventually, I stopped rushing through the work and began taking my time. That change in attitude made the process more enjoyable and turned every day in the garden into a learning experience.

"A garden is a grand teacher. It teaches patience and careful watchfulness; it teaches industry and thrift; above all it teaches entire trust."

— Gertrude Jekyll

Gardening also pushed me to become a careful researcher. I had to learn what seeds to plant, when to plant them, and which soil would help them grow. Without realizing it, I was developing the habit of patient observation and study.

Writing requires the same mindset. Ideas must be nurtured, revised, and reshaped before they are ready to be shared with the world. Just as plants do not grow overnight, meaningful work rarely appears instantly.

Because I had learned to plant seeds in the garden, I understood that my words would also need time to grow. A sentence might become a paragraph. A paragraph might become a chapter. And eventually, with enough patience and persistence, those pages could become a book.

That is how growth works in many areas of life.

If you want to develop patience, consider starting with something simple. Plant a small garden. Buy a houseplant. Care for it consistently and observe how slowly growth unfolds. As the plant develops, you will likely notice that your own patience is developing as well.

"All things come to him who waits, provided he knows what he is waiting for."

— **Woodrow Wilson**

Waiting is often one of the most difficult disciplines in life. Yet patience allows you to remain calm during periods of uncertainty and progress. Many people abandon their goals too early because they expect immediate results.

But the truth is simple: meaningful progress takes time.

Seeds must grow before they produce fruit. Ideas must develop before they become achievements.

Some goals take days to reach. Others take months or even years.

Patience allows you to stay steady during that process.

There will be moments when frustration appears, and quitting feels easier than continuing. In those moments, remember that persistence often separates those who succeed from those who stop too soon.

Keep moving forward.

Success rarely belongs to the fastest person in the room. More often, it belongs to the one who had the patience to continue long enough to see the results of their efforts.

2. Invest in Reading

One of the most valuable investments you can make is developing the habit of reading.

I suggest reading widely in the field you are venturing into—books, articles, essays, research papers, and other reliable sources of knowledge.

Books are powerful because they allow you to learn directly from the experiences, research, and insights of accomplished individuals.

In many ways, reading gives you access to mentors you may never meet in person.

Today, knowledge is more accessible than at any other time in history. Digital libraries, online courses, podcasts, and educational platforms have made learning easier than ever. But the principle remains the same: the more you learn, the more opportunities you are able to recognize.

In the age of artificial intelligence and instant information, the ability to learn continuously has become one of the greatest competitive advantages a person can develop.

You might not have the opportunity to meet influential entrepreneurs, scientists, artists, or innovators in person, but you can still learn from their ideas by reading their books and studying their work. Much of the groundwork has already been done. By reading the work of others, you can study their strategies, understand their mistakes, and apply their insights to your own plans.

Reading not only expands your knowledge—it sharpens your thinking. And occasionally, you may discover that a question you are exploring has not yet been fully answered. When that happens, you are no longer just a reader. You are standing at the frontier of discovery, with the opportunity to contribute new ideas of your own.

The more you read, the more patterns you begin to see—and those patterns often reveal opportunities that others overlook.

3. Invest in Positive Thinking

In today's world, people spend a great deal of time-consuming information—scrolling through social media, watching television, reading news, or listening to music. While these activities can be entertaining or informative, one of the most powerful habits a person can develop is learning how to think positively.

Positive thinking is more than wishful optimism. It is a disciplined way of directing your attention toward possibility rather than limitation.

Throughout history, many successful individuals have shared a similar habit: before they achieved their goals, they first believed that success was possible. They imagined the outcome, focused their thoughts on the opportunity ahead of them, and then acted with confidence.

The way you think has a powerful influence on how you act. Negative thinking often creates hesitation and doubt, while positive thinking encourages initiative and confidence.

When negative thoughts appear—and they will—it is important to recognize them quickly and replace them with more constructive ones. This does not mean ignoring reality. It means choosing a mindset that allows you to move forward rather than remain stuck in fear or self-doubt.

Your thoughts shape your perspective, and your perspective shapes the decisions you make each day.

A simple example illustrates this idea.

Imagine someone who has an idea for a project—a book, a business, or a creative venture. Instead of taking the first step, they begin filling their mind with doubt.

They wonder if their idea is good enough.

They assume someone else has probably already done it better.

They convince themselves that the timing is wrong or that they are not ready.

Over time, those doubts grow stronger than their willingness to act. Eventually the idea is abandoned before it is ever tested.

Months later, they see someone else succeed with a similar idea and wonder what might have happened if they had simply taken the first step.

Situations like this happen more often than people realize. Opportunities are frequently lost not because they were impossible, but because doubt prevented action.

Positive thinking does not guarantee success. But it places your mind in a position to recognize possibilities and act on them.

In a rapidly changing world shaped by technology and automation, the ability to maintain a constructive mindset often determines who adapts to new opportunities and who overlooks them.

When you train your mind to focus on constructive thoughts, your outlook begins to change. Challenges become problems to solve rather than barriers that stop you.

Over time, this mindset strengthens your confidence and helps you move toward the life you want to create.

4. Invest in Focus

Focus is the discipline of directing your attention toward what matters most while ignoring distractions.

Les Brown, one of the world's most renowned motivational speakers, once said:

"Shoot for the moon, and even if you miss, you
will land among the stars; but most people don't
aim too high and miss—they aim too low and
hit."

Focus is the ability to direct your attention toward a clear objective and remain committed to it. Every meaningful achievement begins with identifying a target and concentrating your energy on reaching it.

So, ask yourself a simple question:

What are you aiming for?

Your goal might be to build a business, complete a degree, write a book, master a craft, or become the most productive version of yourself. Whatever the goal may be, progress begins when your attention is directed toward a clear destination.

But in a world filled with constant notifications, distractions, and competing demands for attention, maintaining focus has become more challenging than ever.

Scientific research shows that the human brain is not designed to perform multiple complex tasks at the same time. What we often call "multitasking" is actually task switching—rapidly shifting attention from one task to another.

Studies on task switching have shown that frequently switching between tasks can significantly reduce productivity and increase mental fatigue. When your mind jumps from one activity to another, your brain must repeatedly stop, reset, and refocus.

Over time, these constant interruptions make it harder to maintain deep concentration.

Consider a simple example. Imagine you are working on an important project. Just as you begin making progress, a notification appears on your phone. You check the message, respond quickly, and return to your work—but your mind must now rebuild the same level of concentration you had moments earlier.

Multiply that interruption dozens of times throughout the day, and it becomes clear how easily productivity can decline.

Focus works differently. When you concentrate on one meaningful task at a time, your mind enters a deeper state of engagement. Work becomes clearer, progress becomes faster, and results begin to improve.

Without focus, your goals remain blurry. With focus, your direction becomes clear.

Developing focus requires patience, preparation, and discipline. It is a skill that improves with practice.

The principle is simple: keep your attention focused on what matters most.

When you discipline your attention and direct it toward a meaningful goal, you place yourself in a much stronger position to achieve the things you set out to accomplish.

Where your focus goes, your progress follows.

5. Invest in Eliminating Worry

Everyone wants peace of mind. Most people want to know that their health is stable, their work is secure, and their families are safe. When those things feel uncertain, worry often begins to grow.

But worry rarely improves a situation. In many cases, it only drains the energy needed to solve the problem.

Worry is a mental habit that keeps attention focused on fear rather than solutions.

When the mind becomes consumed with worst-case scenarios, it becomes difficult to think clearly or act confidently.

The truth is that life will always contain uncertainty. Unexpected challenges will appear from time to time.

The goal is not to eliminate every problem, but to develop the ability to respond to them calmly and thoughtfully.

One of the most effective ways to reduce worry is to shift your focus from the problem to the solution.

Instead of asking, "Why is this happening to me?"

Ask, "What can I do next?"

When your attention moves toward action, worry begins to lose its power.

Another important step is learning to release the weight of the past. Holding on to old disappointments, resentment, or regret often keeps the mind trapped in negative cycles of thinking.

Forgiveness—both for others and for yourself—can free mental space and restore clarity.

Peace of mind does not come from living a life without problems. It comes from developing the strength and confidence to face them.

When you focus on solving problems rather than worrying about them, your energy becomes directed toward progress.

And progress, even small progress, gradually replaces worry with confidence.

Worry drains energy.

Action restores it.

Personal Strength

Qualities that shape your character and inner discipline.

6. Invest in Self-Confidence

My grandmother had a very gentle and encouraging spirit. From time to time, she would tell me something that stayed with me:

"What is meant for you, no one can take away."

She didn't say it once or twice. She repeated it over the years until the message eventually settled in my mind. At the time, I didn't fully understand what she was doing. Looking back now, I realize that she was planting confidence in me.

Encouraging words have power. When positive ideas are repeated often enough, they begin to shape the way we think about ourselves and our future. Over time, those thoughts influence our actions and decisions.

That is why building self-confidence is one of the most important investments you can make. If you do not believe in your ability to grow, adapt, and create value, it becomes difficult to pursue any meaningful goal.

Self-confidence is often described as having a realistic belief in your abilities and judgment. In practical terms, it is the quiet inner assurance that you can face challenges, overcome obstacles, and keep moving forward even when progress is slow.

Without self-confidence, many people abandon their goals before they even begin. But with it, individuals are able to push past doubt, fear, and temporary setbacks.

One idea that helped shape my understanding of confidence comes from the work of Napoleon Hill, who wrote extensively about the relationship between thought and belief:

"The subconscious mind will translate into reality a thought driven by fear just as readily as it will translate into reality a thought driven by courage."

In other words, the thoughts you repeatedly entertain eventually influence your actions.

When your mind is filled with doubt, hesitation often follows. But when your thoughts are directed toward growth and possibility, your actions begin to reflect that mindset.

Confidence does not appear overnight. It grows gradually through experience, effort, and small victories over time.

Each challenge you overcome becomes evidence that you are capable of more than you once believed.

When you invest in building self-confidence, you strengthen the foundation that supports every other goal you pursue.

Confidence grows each time you prove to yourself that you are capable of more than you once believed.

7. Invest in Sincerity

Being sincere means expressing your thoughts and intentions honestly and genuinely.

A sincere person communicates with authenticity, speaks truthfully, and acts in ways that reflect their real values.

In everyday life, sincerity can sometimes feel difficult to maintain. People often soften the truth or hide their real thoughts in order to avoid conflict, protect someone's feelings, or make themselves appear more impressive.

Small insincerities may seem harmless, but over time they can weaken trust.

Trust is one of the most valuable forms of social capital a person can build. When people know that your words reflect your true intentions, they are far more likely to respect your judgment, collaborate with you, and support your efforts.

Sincerity also requires honesty with yourself. Recognizing your strengths, acknowledging your weaknesses, and taking responsibility for your actions allows you to grow and improve.

When sincerity becomes part of your character, your reputation becomes stronger. People begin to rely on your word, and that trust can open doors to opportunities that might otherwise remain closed.

In the long run, sincerity is not only a moral virtue—it is a practical advantage.

A sincere person may not always say what others want to hear, but their words carry a kind of credibility that cannot be easily replaced.

8. Invest in Adaptability

The world is constantly changing. Industries evolve, technology advances, and new opportunities appear while others disappear. Because of this, one of the most valuable qualities a person can develop is the ability to adapt.

Adaptability is the willingness to learn, adjust, and grow as circumstances change.

Rather than resisting change, adaptable people learn to recognize the opportunities hidden inside it.

History has shown that those who succeed over the long term are often not the strongest or the most talented, but the ones who are most willing to evolve. They remain curious, open to new ideas, and prepared to adjust their strategies when necessary.

In today's rapidly changing economy—shaped by automation, artificial intelligence, and global connectivity—the ability to adapt has become even more important. Skills that were valuable yesterday may evolve tomorrow, and new tools may transform how work is done.

Rather than fearing these changes, the wiser approach is to learn how to work alongside them. When you remain adaptable, you position yourself to recognize new opportunities as they appear.

Adaptability keeps your thinking flexible and your perspective forward-looking. It allows you to grow with the world instead of being left behind by it.

The future often belongs to those who are willing to evolve with it.

9. Invest in Gratitude

Gratitude is the habit of appreciating what you already have.

It shifts your attention away from what is missing and toward what is present.

When people constantly focus on what they lack, frustration and dissatisfaction tend to grow. But when they take time to appreciate what they already possess—health, knowledge, relationships, and opportunities—their perspective begins to change.

Gratitude does not mean ignoring challenges or pretending that life is perfect.

It simply means recognizing that even during difficult periods, there are still things worth valuing.

A grateful mindset creates emotional balance. It encourages humility, strengthens relationships, and reminds us that progress often comes from building on what we already have.

When gratitude becomes a daily habit, it can transform the way you see the world.

Instead of feeling that life is always withholding something from you, you begin to recognize how much possibility already surrounds you.

Gratitude does not limit ambition—it strengthens the foundation from which ambition grows.

Practical Strength

Habits that help you take action, work well with others, and move ideas forward.

10. Invest in Being Proactive

Being proactive means taking initiative and acting on opportunities instead of waiting for the perfect moment.

Procrastination is the habit of delaying action, often until an opportunity has already passed. If left unchecked, it can quietly prevent people from reaching their goals.

Being proactive is the opposite of procrastination. It means taking initiative, acting on ideas, and moving forward even when circumstances are not perfect.

Many people wait for the "right moment" before taking action. They tell themselves they will begin tomorrow, next week, or when conditions improve. But opportunities rarely wait for perfect timing.

Progress usually begins when someone decides to start with what they have, where they are.

The English writer Charles Dickens once offered simple advice that reflects this principle:

"My advice is to never do tomorrow what you can do today. Procrastination is the thief of time."

Dickens understood the cost of delay. Over the course of his career he produced numerous novels, stories, and essays that continue to influence readers today. Such work requires discipline, consistency, and the willingness to act.

The lesson is simple:

ideas alone do not create results.

Action does.

When you develop the habit of being proactive—starting tasks promptly, addressing problems directly, and moving forward without unnecessary delay—you begin to build momentum. And momentum is one of the most powerful forces behind progress.

Opportunity often rewards the person who begins before everyone else is ready.

But progress rarely happens alone. Turning ideas into meaningful results often requires the support and collaboration of others.

11. Invest in Strong Relationships

Strong relationships are one of the most valuable assets a person can build in life.

When I was in grade school, my mother shared a simple piece of advice with me that stayed in my mind for years:

"To be successful, you have to learn how to get along with other people."

At the time, the lesson seemed small, but over the years I realized how important it truly was.

Success rarely happens in isolation. Most meaningful achievements are the result of cooperation, collaboration, and shared effort.

Teamwork is the coordinated effort of individuals working toward a common goal.

Businesses grow through teams.

Creative projects develop through collaboration.

Even the strongest leaders rely on the support and contributions of others.

Hall of Fame football coach Vince Lombardi captured this idea well when he said:

"Individual commitment to a group effort—that is what makes a teamwork, a company work, a society work, a civilization work."

Learning how to build strong relationships is therefore one of the most valuable investments you can make.

Respect others, communicate clearly, and surround yourself with people who challenge you to grow.

When you work well with others, opportunities multiply, ideas improve, and progress becomes easier to achieve.

Very few accomplishments in life are achieved alone. Strong relationships often turn individual effort into collective success.

12. Invest in Excellence

In everything you do, strive to do it well. Whether you are writing, speaking, designing, building, or serving others, excellence should always be the standard you aim for.

Excellence is reflected in the way you think, the way you communicate, and the care you bring to the work you create.

When you treat others with respect, speak thoughtfully, and take pride in the quality of your work, the results tend to reflect that effort.

Doing things well is more than a professional advantage—it is a personal discipline.

The habits you develop in small actions often shape the larger outcomes of your life.

In the modern economy, the most valuable asset you possess is not a physical object. It is your knowledge, your judgment, and your ability to learn, adapt, and improve.

When you commit yourself to excellence in these areas, you place yourself in a position to grow, create value, and recognize opportunity wherever it appears.

Excellence is not a single achievement. It is a habit practiced over time.

When you commit yourself to doing things well—thinking carefully, acting responsibly, and improving continuously—you place yourself in a position to create value wherever you go.

When you invest in yourself, you build the internal foundation that supports every opportunity you pursue.

Skills improve. Judgment sharpens. Possibilities become easier to recognize.

One of the most powerful investments you can make is investing in your own development.

Chapter 7

Talk the Talk, and Then Walk the Walk

Turning intentions into consistent action

Talking reveals intention. Action creates results.

Ideas, plans, and ambitions all begin with words.

People often talk about what they want to accomplish, what they hope to build, or where they plan to go in life.

Talking about goals can be inspiring, but talking alone does not produce results.

At some point, words must be followed by action.

Many people spend years explaining what they are going to do "someday."

They describe the business they want to start, the book they want to write, or the career they want to build.

But without consistent action, those ideas remain exactly what they started as—ideas.

This is the difference between talking the talk and walking the walk.

Talking the talk is easy. Anyone can describe a vision or announce a plan.

Walking the walk requires discipline, persistence, and the willingness to take the first step even when the outcome is uncertain.

Nothing meaningful happens until movement begins.

Progress rarely appears overnight. It grows through repeated effort—small actions taken consistently over time.

Every successful project, business, or invention began with someone deciding to move from intention to action.

Once action begins, something powerful often follows.

Momentum

Momentum is the force created when consistent action begins to build upon itself. Each step forward makes the next step easier. Progress accelerates because effort is no longer starting from zero.

Think about a high jumper preparing to clear the bar. The athlete does not stand still and leap upward from a dead stop. Instead, the jumper builds speed with a running start. That forward motion creates the momentum needed to clear the obstacle.

The same principle applies to achievement.

Without motion, there is no momentum. Without momentum, progress becomes much harder. But once movement begins, opportunities often appear that were not visible before.

This is why action matters so much. Action creates momentum, and momentum creates progress.

The world around us is filled with examples of people who turned ideas into reality simply because they decided to begin.

Every building, company, book, invention, and technology that exists today is the result of someone choosing to move forward instead of remaining still.

Talking about goals can inspire you, but walking toward those goals is what changes your life.

So, if you have something you want to build, create, or accomplish, start moving toward it. The first step may feel small, but it is often the most important step you will ever take.

Once movement begins, momentum will help carry you forward.

And when momentum builds, the distance between where you are and where you want to go becomes much easier to close.

Chapter 8

Always Make the Right Decision

Letting conscience guide the choices that shape your life

Success in any area of life is largely the result of the decisions we make. Every opportunity, every setback, and every turning point is connected to a choice.

Some decisions move us forward. Others slow us down. And sometimes the most difficult decisions are the ones that determine the direction of our future.

Because of this, learning to make thoughtful decisions is one of the most important skills a person can develop.

Life constantly presents us with choices. Some are small and routine, while others shape the course of our lives. The challenge is not simply making decisions but making decisions with awareness and responsibility.

Before choosing a direction, it helps to pause and ask a few important questions. Will this decision benefit me in the long run, or only in the moment? Will it produce a positive result for the people involved? Is it something I will still feel good about years from now?

Thoughtful questions create thoughtful decisions.

Of course, no one makes perfect decisions all the time. Mistakes happen. Everyone eventually takes a wrong turn somewhere along the journey.

Fortunately, a wrong turn does not mean the journey is over.

Think about how modern navigation systems work. When a driver misses a turn, the system immediately recalculates a new route. One corrected turn leads to another, and before long the driver is back on course.

Life often works in a similar way.

When a mistake is made, the solution is not panic or regret. The solution is to make the next right decision. Then another. And another. A series of better choices gradually places you back on the right path.

In this way, even setbacks can become valuable teachers. They force us to slow down, reflect, and make wiser decisions moving forward.

But there is an even more powerful guide available to us—one that has existed long before any technology was created.

That guide is your conscience.

Your conscience is the quiet inner voice that helps you recognize the difference between what is right and what is wrong. It does not shout or demand attention, but when you learn to listen to it, it can become one of the most reliable guides in your life.

When a decision aligns with your conscience, you often feel a sense of clarity and peace. Your mind becomes calmer, and you are able to move forward without the weight of doubt or regret.

This inner compass becomes stronger the more you learn to trust it.

In many ways, living a productive and meaningful life is not about discovering complicated secrets. It is about consistently making thoughtful decisions and allowing your conscience to guide your direction.

When you do this, you place yourself in a stronger position to recognize opportunity, build trust, and create lasting prosperity.

The decisions we make today do more than shape our immediate circumstances—they determine how prepared we are for the opportunities of tomorrow.

As the world continues to evolve through technology, automation, and new economic systems, the ability to think clearly and choose wisely becomes even more valuable.

The next step is understanding how the modern environment works and how the right tools can multiply the impact of your effort.

Chapter 9

The Shift from Effort to Leverage

How leverage and AI tools multiply opportunity

For most of modern history, economic success was closely tied to effort. People exchanged their time, labor, and physical energy for income. The harder a person worked, the more they expected to earn. This model shaped how many of us were taught to think about opportunity.

But the world is changing.

In today's economy, effort alone is no longer the primary driver of opportunity. Technology, automation, and digital tools have introduced something new into the equation—leverage.

Leverage allows a single idea, skill, or system to produce results far beyond the limits of individual effort. Instead of relying only on the number of hours you can work in a day, tools and intelligent systems can multiply what one person is able to accomplish.

This shift—from effort to leverage—is quietly reshaping how opportunity appears in the modern world.

In the past,
effort created opportunity.

Today,
leverage multiplies it.

Effort starts the engine.

Leverage increases the speed.

What Is Leverage?

In simple terms, leverage is the ability to multiply your effort through tools, systems, and technology.

Instead of relying only on personal labor, leverage allows a single idea, skill, or system to produce results far beyond the limits of individual effort.

In today's digital economy, leverage often appears in the form of:

- software
- digital platforms
- automation
- artificial intelligence tools

These tools allow individuals to produce, distribute, and scale ideas faster than any generation before them.

A single creator can now write, design, build, and publish work that reaches thousands—or even millions—of people around the world.

What once required entire companies or large teams can now be accomplished by individuals who understand how to combine skill, technology, and leverage.

This does not mean that effort no longer matters. Effort is still required. But the nature of effort is evolving.

Modern productivity is no longer measured only by how hard someone works, but also by how intelligently they use the tools available to them.

The environment in which opportunity appears has also changed.

Today's economy is shaped by artificial intelligence, digital platforms, and a global attention economy where ideas can spread instantly.

In this environment, individuals who combine knowledge, creativity, and technology are able to create value at an unprecedented scale.

The principles of opportunity have not changed. But the environment in which those principles operate has evolved.

Hustle opens the door.

Leverage builds the house.

Modern hustle is no longer just about working harder. It is about learning to use intelligent tools, building digital assets, creating systems that work without constant supervision, and owning the channels through which your work reaches the world.

In many ways, this is what hustle evolves into.

Opportunity exists everywhere.

The challenge is that most people fail to see it.

Hustle helps you act on opportunity when it appears. But in the modern economy, hustle alone is no longer enough.

Today, leverage multiplies opportunity—and technology accelerates leverage.

Artificial intelligence, digital platforms, and automated systems allow individuals to accomplish things that once required entire teams. When these tools are used wisely, the results of your effort can expand far beyond the limits of time and labor.

Once you train yourself to recognize value, you will notice something remarkable: there is money all around you.

Opportunity itself is timeless. What changes are the tools we use to capture it.

The principles discussed earlier in this book—**awareness, initiative, self-belief, and resourcefulness**—still apply. But in today's world they increasingly operate through leverage, technology, and digital ownership.

The modern economy is undergoing a quiet transformation.

Effort still matters, but effort alone is no longer the primary driver of opportunity.

Tools, systems, and intelligent technologies are changing how work is performed and how value is created.

Today, a single individual with the right tools can accomplish what once required teams of people.

This is the shift from effort to leverage.

Understanding this shift is the first step. The next step is learning how leverage operates in the modern economy—and how new technologies are expanding what individuals are capable of creating.

Chapter 10

Opportunity in the Age of Automation

The people who create the greatest opportunities are not always the ones who work the hardest. They were often the ones who understood how to use leverage.

Effort builds momentum.

Leverage multiplies results.

Leverage allows a single idea, skill, or system to produce results far beyond the limits of individual effort. In the past, leverage was often reserved for large organizations with access to capital, machinery, and labor.

Today, that reality is changing.

Digital platforms, intelligent software, and artificial intelligence tools have placed unprecedented leverage into the hands of individuals.

A writer can publish globally from a laptop.

A creator can reach millions through a single platform.

A small team can build systems that once required entire companies.

In the modern economy, the question is no longer whether leverage exists. The real question is whether you know how to use it.

Leverage often appears in three powerful forms.

Technology leverage

Artificial intelligence tools, automation, and software systems that expand what a single individual can produce.

Platform leverage

Digital platforms, online marketplaces, and internet distribution systems that allow ideas, products, and services to reach global audiences.

Knowledge leverage

Skills, systems, and intellectual property that allow expertise and ideas to generate value beyond the limits of physical labor.

By now you have seen that opportunity rarely arrives with a loud announcement. Most of the time it appears quietly—hidden inside knowledge, discipline, relationships, and the decisions we make each day.

Some people spend their lives waiting for opportunity to knock on their door. Others eventually realize that opportunity has been standing beside them the entire time.

The difference is awareness.

When you train your mind to recognize value, opportunity begins to appear in places that once seemed ordinary. An idea becomes a business. A skill becomes income. A financial tool becomes leverage. A disciplined habit becomes long-term prosperity.

None of these things happen by accident. They happen when knowledge, discipline, and action work together.

Throughout this book, the goal has been simple: to help you recognize that the ability to create value already exists within you.

Once you understand that truth, the world begins to look different.

Problems start to resemble opportunities, and obstacles begin to reveal possible solutions.

Opportunity has always surrounded those who are prepared to recognize it.

Sometimes it appears as a new idea.

Sometimes it appears as a lesson learned from failure.

Sometimes it appears as a tool you already possess but have not yet learned to use.

The people who prosper are not necessarily the luckiest people. They are often the ones who learn to see possibilities where others see limitations.

Throughout this book you have seen that prosperity does not begin with money. It begins with the habits, mindset, and character you develop within yourself. When those qualities are cultivated, opportunity becomes easier to recognize.

The tools may change. The environment may evolve. But the principle remains the same:

opportunity still surrounds those who are prepared to see it.

So, wherever you go from here—continue learning, continue growing, and continue looking closely at the world around you.

Because if you truly take a look…

you will discover that there is opportunity,

possibility,

and prosperity

all around you.

Final Thoughts

Opportunity rarely announces itself in obvious ways. Most of the time it appears quietly—inside ideas, lessons, relationships, and the decisions we make each day.

Some people spend years searching for opportunity somewhere far away. Others eventually realize that opportunity has been near them all along.

The difference is awareness.

When you begin to look carefully at your skills, your knowledge, your experiences, and the tools available around you, you start to see possibilities that once seemed invisible.

The truth is simple: opportunity often exists in places we overlook.

All it takes is the willingness to look a little closer.

Take a closer look.

You may discover more possibilities than you ever imagined.

Before You Go

Thank you for taking the time to read this book.

If the ideas in these pages helped you see opportunity from a new perspective, consider leaving a short review on Amazon. Reviews help other readers discover the book and allow these ideas to reach more people.

Your support is greatly appreciated.

If you found this book helpful, please consider sharing it with someone who might benefit from it.

Opportunity is still everywhere.

Learn to recognize it.

One Final Question

Now that you have finished this book, take a moment and ask yourself one simple question:

What opportunity around me have I been overlooking?

The answer to that question may be the beginning of your next chapter.

About the Author

Photo by A.D.A. Studios

Zangba Thomson is an award-winning author, journalist, and digital publisher. His writing explores opportunity, culture, and creative independence in the modern era.

His work has been featured across major media outlets including FOX 5, NBC, ABC, Essence Magazine, Vibe Magazine, and international publications such as the *Daily Mail* (UK), reaching audiences across multiple platforms.

To explore more writing and future projects, visit:

ZangbaThomson.com

"In every generation the tools change, but the principle remains the same: those who learn to recognize opportunity and act on it will always discover that value—and often prosperity—exists all around them." — **Zangba Thomson**

Zangba Thomson is the founder of Bong Mines Entertainment, an independent media platform dedicated to discovering emerging artists and documenting global music culture.

Continue the Journey

If you enjoyed this book and would like to explore more ideas about opportunity, creativity, and building value in the modern economy, visit:

BongMinesEntertainment.com

There you'll find writing on music, culture, emerging artists, and creative work shaping the modern landscape.

Thank you for reading.

And remember:

There is always opportunity for those who learn to recognize it.

www.ingramcontent.com/pod-product-compliance
Lightning Source LLC
Chambersburg PA
CBHW021338060726
47591CB00006B/2072